GOOD DOGS ONLY

REBECCA FELIX

Lerner Publications ◆ Minneapolis

Lerner Publications Company
An imprint of Lerner Publishing Group, Inc.
241 First Avenue North
Minneapolis, MN 55401 USA

For reading levels and more information, look up this title at www.lernerbooks.com.
Main body text set in Caecilia Com
Typeface provided by Monotype

Library of Congress Cataloging-in-Publication Data

Names: Felix, Rebecca, 1984– author.
Title: Good dogs only / Rebecca Felix.
Description: Minneapolis : Lerner Publications, [2021] | Series: Internet animal stars | Includes bibliographical references and index. | Audience: Ages 6–10 | Audience: Grades 2–3 | Summary: "Acquaint young readers with everybody's best friend, the dog! Curricular content includes details of their life cycle and habitat, showcased within an engaging social-media-inspired design"— Provided by publisher.
Identifiers: LCCN 2019052406 (print) | LCCN 2019052407 (ebook) | ISBN 9781541597167 (library binding) | ISBN 9781728402888 (paperback) | ISBN 9781728400365 (ebook)
Subjects: LCSH: Dogs—Juvenile literature.
Classification: LCC SF426.5 .F47 2021 (print) | LCC SF426.5 (ebook) | DDC 636.7—dc23

LC record available at https://lccn.loc.gov/2019052406
LC ebook record available at https://lccn.loc.gov/2019052407

Manufactured in the United States of America
1 – CG – 7/15/20

#HotDog

PAGE PLUS

Scan QR codes throughout the book for videos of cute animals!

GOOD DOGS ONLY

What do you know about dogs? They are in the canine family. Dogs are related to gray wolves! But unlike wolves, dogs live with and around humans. Dogs entertain humans too. The internet is full of goofy dogs. Dig into dog facts. Then discover how and why pups earned online fame!

#WhoaDoggies

There are more than 300 dog breeds.

#GoodBoy

Chapter 1

DOG DAYS

★ Wee Pups ★

Baby dogs are puppies. They can be many sizes! This depends on their **breed**.

Newborn puppies cannot see or hear. They sleep often. Within a few weeks, puppies gain their senses.

Puppies walk at four weeks old. Then they play!

Puppies wrestle, romp, and nip.

Scan this QR code to see a playful puppy!

★ Grown-Ups ★

After two to three months, puppies can be adopted as pets. They keep playing and growing.

Many puppies gain half their body weight by five months.

By age two, a dog is full size.

Dogs age more quickly than humans. How quickly **varies**. Large dogs age fastest.

#PupPower

★ Elder Dogs ★

Dog adulthood lasts five to ten years. Some older dogs remain **energetic**. But many slow down as they age.

Many dogs are social. Some are timid. Others are goofy. Dog behavior varies. But all dogs have the same needs.

#PetPup

There are more than seventy-five million pet dogs in the United States!

Chapter 2

PACKS & SNACKS

Dogs live all around the world! Wherever dogs live, it's in their nature to join a pack.

Dogs seek time around other dogs and people. Many dogs **bond** with their owners.

Dogs also need down time. Give them a comfortable space to be alone. This could be a cozy dog bed or crate!

Dogs are smart and athletic. Give them toys to solve, chase, or chew.

Most dogs eat prepared food. But their teeth are made for hunting.

Scan this QR code to see some stellar dog tricks!

Give dogs toys and bones to gnaw.

Lots of dogs love treats! Don't overfeed dogs, though. Being chunky is a big health problem for pups.

Exercise keeps dogs healthy.
Take dogs for runs or walks
in a dog park! Pet experts say
a tired dog is a good dog . . .

. . . but the internet says all dogs are good dogs! Happy dogs charm the online world.

So do silly dogs,
sweet dogs,
and skilled dogs!

Chapter 3

DOGS IN POP CULTURE

Dogs are in the internet's most popular posts. But how and why did dogs become famous online?

In 2015, social media account WeRateDogs began rating pictures of people's pet dogs. It gave each one a super high score. Soon, dogs began to rule the internet!

Smartphones also helped dogs become internet famous. These gadgets let dog owners post high-quality videos and photographs of their dogs.

Experts also think dogs are popular for their personalities. Dogs are **loyal** and loving. This brings people **comfort**. Many people just think dogs are adorable!

#PupStar

★ Top Dogs ★

Dogs become online stars for many reasons. Some star in a single **viral** post. Others have their own social media accounts, websites, and more!

Scan this QR code to see a laptop-loving dog!

Superstar! ★
DOUG THE PUG

Doug the Pug was born in 2012. He has millions of social media followers. Companies have made books and toys featuring Doug. He has also starred in music videos!

MEME BREAK!

WHEN YOU TRY TO MAKE BREAKFAST BY YOURSELF

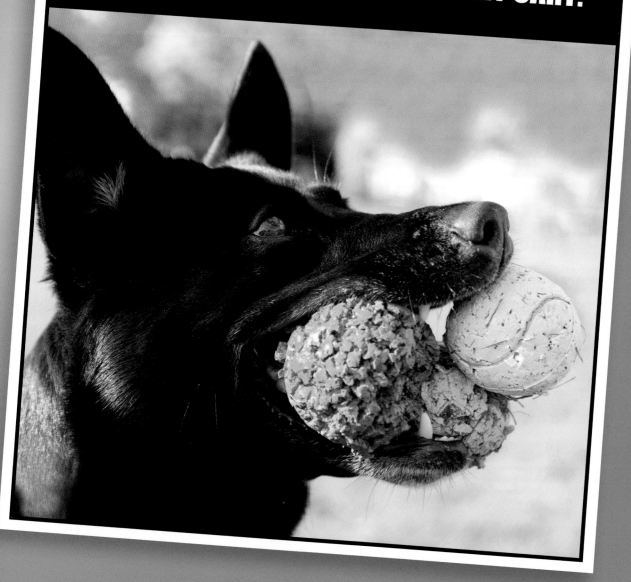

MOM: YOU CAN PICK ONE BOX OF CEREAL. ME COMING BACK TO THE GROCERY CART:

DOGS ROCK!

Canine **content** is wildly popular. It even **impacts** language! Online posts call dogs "doggos," "puppers," and "good boys." These terms are now used around the world.

Online puppers also encourage pet adoption and rescue. And dogs with disabilities and unique looks **inspire** acceptance.

Dogs are loved worldwide.

bond: a strong, positive feeling that forms a connection between living things

breed: a particular kind of animal

comfort: a feeling of ease and relief

content: ideas, facts, and images available online

energetic: having a lot of energy

impact: to affect something

inspire: to cause someone to want to do something

loyal: having or showing full support for someone or something

viral: spreading quickly to many people over the internet

WEBSITES

DK Find Out—Domestic Dogs
https://www.dkfindout.com/us/animals-and-nature/dogs/domestic-dogs/
Find tons of facts about dogs, including their origin, breeds, and more.

Ducksters—Dogs
https://www.ducksters.com/animals/dogs.php
Explore dog breeds and behaviors, learn how to choose a pet dog, and more.

National Geographic Kids—Dog Science Unleashed
https://kids.nationalgeographic.com/explore/books/dog-science/
Complete activities that teach the science behind dog paw preferences and sniffing!

BOOKS

Fiedler, Heidi. *Wacky Things Pets Do: Weird & Amazing Facts about Pets!* Lake Forest, CA: Walter Foster Jr./Quarto, 2018.
Read about the surprising, silly, and sometimes gross behaviors of dogs and other pets.

Mosier, Leslie. *I Am Doug the Pug.* New York: Scholastic, 2019.
Learn how Doug the Pug became an internet celebrity and what his daily life is like. Check out Doug photos and complete Doug-related activities!

Schuh, Mari C. *The Supersmart Dog.* Minneapolis: Lerner Publications, 2019.
Discover dogs that know tons of commands, perform tricks, and have even learned to do simple math!